JURASSIC SHARK

PAINTINGS BY KAREN CARR · WRITTEN BY DEBORAH DIFFILY

A BYRON PREISS BOOK
HarperCollinsPublishers

This book is dedicated with love to my father, Bill Carr,
who had a tough year but has come through just fine.
—K.C.

ACKNOWLEDGMENTS
I would like to express tremendous appreciation to Commander Zim,
Howard Zimmerman at Byron Preiss Publications, for his infinite
patience and professional support. And a Jurassic-sized "thank you"
goes to my editors at HarperCollins for their
continuing assistance and support.
—K.C.

Editor: Howard Zimmerman
Interior design: Gilda Hannah
Jacket designer: Stephanie Bart-Horvath
Typeset in Caxton
The art in this book was created using Corel Paint software.

A Byron Preiss Book

Jurassic Shark
Jurassic Shark copyright © 2004 by Byron Preiss Visual Publications, Inc.
Illustrations copyright © 2004 by Karen Carr
Manufactured in China by South China Printing Company Ltd.
All rights reserved.
www.harperchildrens.com

Library of Congress Cataloging-in-Publication Data
Carr, Karen.
Jurassic Shark / paintings by Karen Carr, written by Deborah Diffily.
p.   cm.
Summary: Profiles Hybodus, a fearless and deadly prehistoric shark, looking at her feeding
habits, preparations for giving birth, and dangers to herself and her baby.
ISBN 0-06-008249-6 — ISBN 0-06-008250-x (lib. bdg.)
[1. Hybodus—Juvenile literature. [1. Sharks, Fossil. 2. Prehistoric animals.] I. Title.
Qe852.E6 2004   2002152614
567'.3—dc21

1 2 3 4 5 6 7 8 9 10
❖
First Edition

Hybodus.
Rows of razor-sharp teeth,
seven feet of muscle . . .
she lived 180 million years ago.

Hybodus is the deadliest shark in the sea.
She swims alone. She is fearless.
She will attack anything, no matter how big.

Hybodus senses *Elasmosaurus* is nearby.
Elasmosaurus is forty-five feet long—a meat eater.
Elasmosaurus is strong enough to kill *Hybodus*.

But *Hybodus* is fearless. She strikes again and again.
When *Elasmosaurus* is dead, *Hybodus* eats until she is full.
Soon other predators will come, drawn by the blood of *Elasmosaurus*.

Hybodus's hunts are not always successful.
This school of ichthyosaurs chase *Hybodus* away
when she tries attacking one of their young.

Hybodus never stops looking for food.
When she spies a school of squid, she swims toward them.
Her jaws open wide.
Her muscles propel her body through the water.
Her jaw snaps shut on the squid, ripping through their flesh.
Her jaws and teeth fold inward to force the meat to her stomach.

In the shallow water nearby, a herd of *Camptosaurs* is wading.
Hybodus swims closer. She is still hungry.
Other predators attack. But today *Hybodus* does not.

Hybodus is going to have a baby.
Until her baby is born, she will avoid bloody battles.
While she hunts for food, she searches for a safe place to give birth.

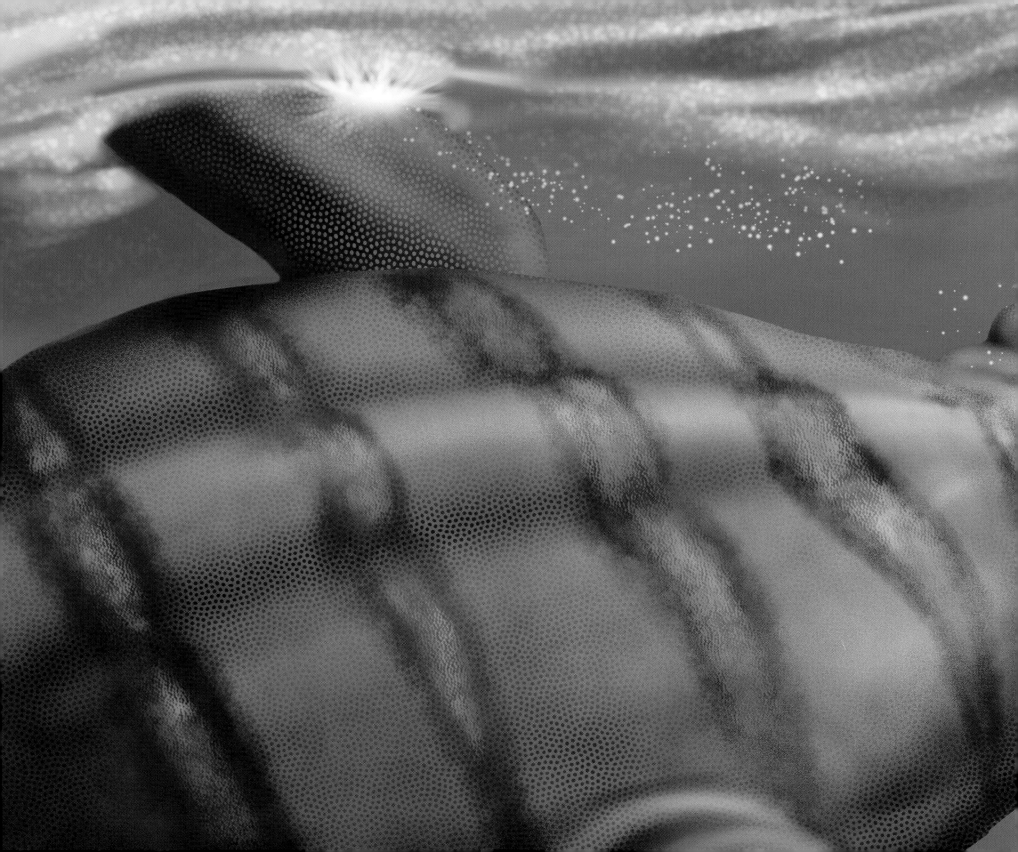

Hybodus finds a safe place among the coral reefs.
She can have her baby there.
But above her, there is danger.

Liopleurodon is eighty feet long.
He weighs many tons. His jaws are ten feet wide.
His teeth are like knives.

Liopleurodon is the largest animal in the Jurassic seas.
His enormous flippers pull him through the water with great speed.
He swims after the school of ichthyosaurs that earlier had chased *Hybodus* away.

Hybodus swims into the school of frightened ichthyosaurs.
She chooses one.
She strikes.

Before she can feed on her victim, *Liopleurodon* swims over.
He is big enough and strong enough to steal *Hybodus*'s food.
Hybodus knows this. She swims away, still hungry.
Hybodus is angry. She is a predator. The ichthyosaur was hers.

Hybodus knows that *Liopleurodon* is dangerous.
Hybodus knows that her baby will not be safe when he
is in her territory.

Her instincts tell her to be careful, but to attack.
She swims up to *Liopleurodon* while he is feeding and
quickly bites a hunk of flesh from behind his front flipper.

Liopleurodon's blood fills the water.
Quickly, other predators arrive. They are attracted by
the scent of fresh blood.
Liopleurodon is injured. He can't fight them off.
They attack, and *Liopleurodon* is dead within minutes.

Hybodus has made the area safe for her baby.
She swims to the coral reef she found and gives birth.

The baby shark is born alive, and hungry.
She swims around her mother for a few minutes, and
then the baby swims away to search for food.

Hunt or be hunted, kill or be killed,
the Jurassic seas were a dangerous place.
Today, *Hybodus* defeated an enemy ten times her size.
Today, the predator became the prey.
Today, *Hybodus* was the victor,
the deadliest shark in the Jurassic seas.

CAST OF CHARACTERS

Ichthyosaurs
ik-THE-o-sawrs

Elasmosaurus
e-LAS-mo-SAWR-us

Liopleurodon
LIE-o-PLOOR-o-don

Hybodus
HIE-bod-dus